About the Author

Sara Joy Warne is a psychic advisor and counselor in Las Vegas, Nevada. She is a singer/songwriter and author. She is a proud mother of three amazing teenagers.

The Spell Book of Magick Poems

Sara Joy Warne

The Spell Book of Magick Poems

Vanguard Press

VANGUARD PAPERBACK

© Copyright 2024
Sara Joy Warne

The right of Sara Joy Warne to be identified as author of
this work has been asserted by them in accordance with the
Copyright, Designs and Patents Act 1988.

All Rights Reserved

No reproduction, copy or transmission of this publication
may be made without written permission.
No paragraph of this publication may be reproduced,
copied or transmitted save with the written permission of the
publisher, or in accordance with the provisions
of the Copyright Act 1956 (as amended).

Any person who commits any unauthorised act in relation to
this publication may be liable to criminal
prosecution and civil claims for damages.

A CIP catalogue record for this title is
available from the British Library.

ISBN 978 1 80016 890 9

This is a work of fiction. Names, characters, businesses, places, events and
incidents are either the product of the author's imagination or used in a
fictitious manner. Any resemblance to actual persons, living or dead, or
actual events is purely coincidental.

Vanguard Press is an imprint of
Pegasus Elliot Mackenzie Publishers Ltd.
www.pegasuspublishers.com

First Published in 2024

Vanguard Press
Sheraton House Castle Park
Cambridge England

Printed & Bound in Great Britain

I dedicate this book to Beth, and to all other poetic witches, here to help heal this crazy, wounded world in perfect love and perfect trust.

"Magick is the art of causing changes in consciousness to occur in accordance with the will."
DION FORTUNE

Contents

Foreword	13
The Call of Magick	14
Acknowledging the Call	15
When the North Winter Ends	17
Acknowledging the Element Earth	19
It's going to be a Witchy Night	21
Acknowledging the Element Air	23
The Flames that are brought to Light	26
Acknowledging the Element Fire	27
The Watery Place	30
Acknowledging the Element Water	31
You are the Fifth Element	34
Acknowledging the Element of Ether	35
A Woman's Anthem	38
Covens and Gatherings	43
Existence	47
Casting Your Circle and Calling the Corners	49
Never Burn Again	52
Invoking the Moon Goddess	55
Not so Trendy Witch	57
Cleansing and Protecting	61
A Gift and It's in the Blood	67
Blood and Sex Magick	69
Shadow	71
Shadow Work	73
A Witch Will Get Ya Back	80
Candle Magick	82
The Day of the Dead	86

Honoring the Deceased on Halloween	89
It's Up to Us Now	94
17 Second Manifestation	96
Ask Yourself Witch, Have You Made Your Mark?	99
Final Thoughts	101
Spell Dictionary, Keywords and Appendix	105

Foreword

Attempt to be prophetic. The power of words is simply magical. While I do want you to read and enjoy all of the poems that I have written, my main purpose is to inspire and encourage you to write poems of your own. Manifest, create, and contribute to the many other wounded souls that too so long to heal. Your words are medicine. They are shamanistic and personal, and can do so much in your life. After every witchy poem you will read, I include a spell to tie in with it. These spells are both traditional and modern, and suitable for every type of witch. Whether you are new to magick or familiar with the craft, these words should resonate with you as if you lived life in my shoes. We all walk a similar path as wise witches. So write, my dear friend. Write about all your pain, your joy, and your hope for your spirit and for the other souls that can also relate to your experiences. It is the poems and the spells you create that will transform into beauty. So read and write on; the universe is calling you.

Blessed be.

Sara Joy Warne

The Call of Magick

The call of magick speaks so true
It has no way of ever warning you
It knows just what it needs you to achieve
And when it pulls you in, you suddenly believe.

It's the sudden, instant chill you feel
The kind that only you know to be real
It's the whisper in your ear so light
It could be heard in the wind at night.

All of us witches know the sensation
To be summoned without invitation
To witness the things you can't explain
To howl at the moon and dance in the rain.

There's no time like the here and now
To allow yourself to be involved, somehow
You will know the exact moment in your heart
The call of magick needs you to do your part.

Acknowledging the Call

Spell Work #1

Attempt to be wild. Go out and into as close to being a part of nature as you can. This can even be a part of your own backyard, but a beach, forest, or desert is always ideal. This practice works any time of the day or night, and within all of the wonderful seasons. Begin your solitude and adventure by paying attention to your newfound surroundings. Look for things around you, in your environment, that speak to you. As if these items are personally gifted from the universe especially for you, so gather these items. They can be leaves, stones, paper and flower petals, whatever speaks to you. As you gather your presents from the Faes, feel the energy of every single item as it is held in your hand. Then, place each item together and give them safety in their own chosen box, jar, or bag. Close your eyes, and let your audible senses take over. Listen for anything that might become your confirmation that you are exactly where you should be, at the exact moment you have found yourself there. Hear birds, the whining of the breeze, insects, even unfamiliar sounds that you might not recognize. These are all sounds that connect you in spirit to the beautiful world around you. Mother Nature will protect you in her arms and will understand what you have come for. This brand new source of enlightenment will grant you with your own divination. Thank the gods for the exchange you have made with your items and then return home to your sacred space or where you can utilize your new treasures undisturbed.

You now have found your own personal runes, handcrafted from the earth and handpicked by you. Toss these items and pay attention to the positions they lie in and the sequences and patterns they create in their unity together. Cherish these nature runes, and they will never let you down when it comes to guidance into foreseeing what is in store for your future. You have just acknowledged the call of magick, and made it a new practiced magick of your own divinity. Now, the boundaries are limitless, as the veil is opened. If possible, create your own poetic words from your experiences with this spell. So shall it be.

When the North Winter Ends

When the sting of January is leaving, and the earth element transcends
This I am certain in my sadness is when the north winter ends.

As I see that every leaf is broken pieces of dust, scattered on the ground
As I hear in the night, birds barely can be heard making a sound.

There is stillness all around me, and I am too cold to move too much
There's a dreary fog above me, yet still no release of snow to touch.

The numbness in my fingertips makes it harder to use my hands
The warm breath I blow on my skin is all my body understands.

Despite my cherry, icy nose and my teary, squinted eyes
I'm not quite ready to tell this fading season my goodbyes.

Yet acceptance is one thing that winter has taught me, among other things
I have evolved and been taught many lessons, that is what this season brings.

I am grateful, I am still ever changing, and open to what may come
I am ready to kiss the crisp air and allow this merry time to be done.

I will forever remember the songs, the laughter, and cider scented fumes
I will cherish the moments I found comfort snuggling, and sleeping until noon.

I am a matured, wiser woman, a mother who can relate to this earth
And I have a deeper understanding of my place here and how much I am worth.

So I will whisper to myself and the world around me a "Thank you" as I turn
I will face the direction of the new and fresh fire I will burn.

I will sit and reflect about every meaningful day that has passed
Knowing that I may be chilly, right now, but the air of spring is approaching fast.

Acknowledging the Element Earth

Spell Work #2

Attempt to be grounded. Walk in the dirt with bare feet, touch leaves and crystals, plant a seed with care. These things tie into the beloved element of earth. It is the direction of north and the season of winter. It is represented by the witches of the astrological signs Taurus, Virgo and Capricorn. Earth is the head mother of nature and trust. She is nurturing, thorough and hearty. The Goddess of the North is the crone who knows exactly what warm soup to feed you, to warm your belly when it's cold outside. Be in sync with this wise witch in whatever ways you feel are suitable. Be creative and design your own personal manifestation or craft to align with her. You will not go unnoticed, and you will thrive in the qualities that earth represents in the balance of the four corners. These qualities are strong, practical, connected, and universal.

Spread out some seeds or some soil at your feet. Begin to feel earth even more present, and stand in the direction of the north. Lift your hands up to the sky and recite these words. "I thank you, Mother Earth, and I acknowledge all of your blessings. Protect me. I am here and I am whole. So bless it be." You will feel the importance of this element and it will come in handy soon, when you cast your circle and call the corners. This is when your true and personal magick will be created, and you will find yourself one with all of the elements. When you are ready, cook a savory meal, be crafty with art, or even organize and declutter. These things are ways we honor and become one with the element of earth. If you feel the need, once again write about your experiences flourishing with this element. Your words are your own personal magick words, and just as powerful as words from any sacred texts. The words you write are your sacred truths, and they will mark history for you and others to come. So shall it be.

It's going to be a Witchy Night

Springtime is near and I find myself drawn to the full moon light
I go outside knowing it's going to be a witchy night
The moment I feel the sensation of the wind on my skin
I can't help but be hypnotized and mystically, I am taken in.

The gusts swarm me and pique my awareness fast
I hear the sound of the wind knocking over and breaking a glass
I surrender to the power of the storm that's brewing
I understand just what Mother East is doing.

She is singing to me and yet being a reminder
That she was never gone, even though I couldn't find her
Winter is over and she has returned with much to give
And I know how to be one with her in the way that I live.

Tonight may be witchy but there is much joy to gain
There will be storms to nourish the seeds to grow from the rain
Once each blossomed bud or born baby is seen and felt

I will think of new beginnings and watch the ice quickly melt.

It will be colorful days, with busyness and love everywhere
I can smell honeysuckles and misty clouds in the air
So I will be silent and in awe, through this amazing, witchy night
For I know that the darkness will be broken with the morning light.

Acknowledging the Element Air

Spell Work # 3

Attempt to flow. On a windy day – during the season of spring would be perfect (yet not necessary) – stand in the east. This manifestation spell will get you acquainted with the air element. Air is represented by the east direction and holds the beauty tied in with springtime and new beginnings. The astrological signs are Gemini, Libra and Aquarius. The element air is what allows us as witches and human beings to let go. This element carries characteristics consisting of being dreamy, childlike, curious and intelligent. It is the Goddess of the East that ties in with the faerie realm and knows magick work with elementals, as it comes so naturally. This goddess reminds us to see the world with the eyes of a child, or to go into the forest and embrace nature. She is a symbol of the cycles, new birth and youth. She will come in handy when you do this spell honoring her element.

The key to this manifestation is to let go of something that is taking up too much space in your life, where new miracles are trying to come in. So on this windy day you choose – think of something that is in need of releasing, that has been held on to for much too long. I am referring to emotional or spiritual or even psychological attachments that are holding you back as a person. This can be releasing fear of success, or letting go of the hope for a relationship to get better when it is toxic in your life. It can be releasing the mourning of a loved one that has passed, even letting go of old patterns that you recognize to be unfulfilling in your lifestyle. This is your spell so whatever your release, get ready to set it free. Now decide on a tangible item represented by this element that will represent what you are about to set free. These items include light feathers or also smoke from the smolder of a snuffed yellow candle or incense of your choice. Now as you stand at the east, hold either your feather up high towards the wind gusts or allow your smoke to rise high, catching the heavy breeze. Either way or both ways can be done, but the importance is watching the item until the wind takes it to where it can no longer be seen in the distance any more. As you watch the wind free the feather or carry the smoke, picture what it is you are letting go of being taken with it. Let the winds allow it to be placed wherever the universe needs it to be. It is now out of your hands, away from your sight, and out of your life. Allow the wind to whoosh up against you for as long as you feel it should. During this time, visualize with every brush of it that you are closer to the new replacement. This is due to the spell that has just made more room in your life. You have just freed something and made a strong effort that will soon be rewarded. You have cleared the space allowing a new blessing to appear in your life.

There is space now for this blessing to fit, and remember to manifest your heart's desire at this time. Air does represent new transitions and beginnings in your life. Miracles are now ready to happen, and seeds that you plant in your conscious reality will blossom with strong roots and many flowers. As soon as you feel it's time or when you are confirmed by the heavy wind's sudden settle, say "I allow what is no longer needed to be set free. As I will it so shall it be!" If you feel like journaling about this, because it can be very emotional and liberating, feel free to write in your book of shadows about your experience and how it felt. Also, remember to write on about the aftermaths of this powerful spell's magick. You will love to tell the tale later on, about the ways this spell has manifested and brought new joys in your life. So bless it be.

The Flames that are brought to   Light

I am the flames that burn and smolder
I bring warmth to the earth as it gets colder.

I am the summer, the throbbing heat
The red coals that leave blisters beneath the feet.

I am the Goddess of the South appearing in a smoky haze
Causing the scorching, shifting, cosmic blaze.

I am the daring truth that brings forth desire
I am the power to cleanse as the element fire.

I am creative forces of powerful energy you feel
I know freedom is the way for the spirit to heal.

I'll guide you to the strength that you had as a child
Reminding you of your ancient ways to be wild.

So dance with the rhythm and let my fire ignite
Any parts of you begging to be brought to light.

Acknowledging the Element Fire

Spell Work #4

Attempt to be fierce. If you are able, go somewhere where a bonfire can be lit. Light the fire while standing in the direction of the south. Or if you cannot be around a fire, light a candle (preferably red). Fire is the south direction and the season of summer. It is represented by the astrological signs Aries, Leo and Sagittarius. This flame you will ignite will create the spell to get you into the flow with this element. It will make you comfortable knowing that fire is powerful and deadly, yet more importantly it is what provides warmth and is the center of our life forces. Fire carries the characteristics from the south goddess that mainly include creativity, energy and sexual connection. Fire is what creates the unapologetic and wild parts of every witch. It gives us confidence, lust, and the ability to conquer all that we desire.

After you have decided on a bonfire or a single candle flame, find the ability and the space somehow to dance. You may choose to use a wand or staff to make a circle surrounding your sacred space, in order to lock in the creative frequencies in which your dance will take place. Or you may choose not to. The fire element, when setting up an altar, is represented by wood, branches, or an asthame or wand, so this can work beautifully.

(These items also make wonderful and unique dancing props.)

As you light your small or large flame, say these words or something similar you create on your own. "I light this flame in the power of the south to honor the element fire; now as I dance, I will manifest all that I desire. So bless it be!" Focus your vision on the flame. Notice it begin to flicker or brighten, as if the flame is dancing. Absorb that vibrant energy as you feel it in your solar plexus. Now dance with your ignited flame. Dance around the flame as your center, and hold a wish in your thoughts. This is your manifestation dance, and you can do this to your favorite songs or while chanting; you can add drums or other instruments, or dance beautifully in silence. This is your dancing spell, so the choice is up to you. The more you dance, the more power you are raising to bring forth your wish. Feel yourself become the goddess that you are, beautiful in your every motion. You are as potent as a Native American dancing to bring the rain. Enjoy this time, and try your best to not hold back or fear what you might be dancing like. There are no wrong moves in your fire magick. When you begin to get tired or when your flickering flame becomes fragile, calm down your energy and focus on the flame as you snuff it. As you watch the smoke rise up to the sky, trust that it is putting your wish into motion and sending your energies and manifestation into the universe. Find a way to dance as much as you can and write about these wonderful, creative moments in your book of shadows. This is powerful and fiery spell work. Have fun. And so it shall be.

The Watery Place

When you find yourself lost out in space,
Find yourself again home at the nearest watery place

In the direction of the west, the soul is often seen
By the Cancer, Scorpio, or Pisces Queen

You may hear the waves nearby hitting the shore
Or you may dream about the depths of the ocean's floor

The water is the mystical and mysterious salvation
That is so limitless in its soothing concentration

It is the watery places where peace is found
Where intuition and emotion swarms you all around

With the flow of a stream in constant motion
With the tear as it trickles from sheer devotion

As it gathers as a raindrop that falls from the sky
Or as it replenishes your throat, thirsty and dry

Water lets us swim, rinse, bathe, and play,
And reminds us to respect autumn in a holy way

Every aspect that this element holds with grace
Are all the reasons you will find me, at the watery place

Acknowledging the Element Water

Spell Work #5

Attempt to revitalize. This spell is to not only familiarize you with the element water, but also to replenish and recycle your own being. Water is for the direction of the west and the season of autumn. It is represented by the last three astrological signs, Cancer, Scorpio and Pisces. The water element is what restores a witch's soul and the soul of the earth. We are linked to this element by our intuition, emotions, and artistic abilities. Water is what nurtures, cleanses, and restores all that is drained or in need of nourishment. It is the Goddess of the West that teaches us about transitions, and the importance of life and death and its eternal cycle. This water spell is a perfect spell to use after feeling too spiritually or physically drained. It is also great to get rid of unwanted, leftover energies. This spell is also ideal for what you, as the psychic witch you are, might need after a long stretch of using your gift of divination and healing others. The point of it is to recycle the old and replace what is no longer needed with a new and recharged alignment. Any time of the day or night of the year is the right time for this spell. So use it as needed.

Get in the shower. Adjust everything to your liking. Be as calm and as centered as possible. Use this as your meditation, only equipped with your personal favorite scents, lathered soaps, music, candles, etc. As you are enjoying the divine water as it hits your body, pay attention to the power of the water. Visualize every drop, every single bit of the water you are feeling, as pure, positive energy. Visualize the stream of water as joy, confidence, rebirth, replenishment, and peace. Now turn your focus to the drain at your feet. Watch every bit of water that has rolled off your body, below you, as it vanishes. Visualize all the negative energy from that day disappearing. Watch it as it goes down the drain. Know that all that has drained you is over, and being replaced by the new water that is cleansing and purifying your body. You can get as deep into this recycling, mediation spell as you wish. Wash your face, with eyes closed, so all you have seen throughout the day is washed away. As you wash your hair, picture all negativity that has entered your presence and latched on to your hair now falling at your feet. As you wash your hands, visualize yourself scrubbing away all that you have touched. Even as you wash your feet, wipe away all that you have stepped across that you no longer wish to carry with you. All of these parts about anything you are rinsing, you will then witness getting sucked down the drain. If you wish, say these words. "Water of magick, replenish me from head to toe. All that is negative I will now let go! So bless it be!"

As a follow up, I like to dry my body afterwards with uplifting intentions. I do this by focusing all of the positive thoughts and feelings that I am manifesting into the new day that I am approaching. I am ready to face the world now with grace. I will think happy thoughts as I dry my hair, and visualize myself in a pure state of bliss as I dry my entire body. This spell really makes me feel amazing, and I know you will love it too. Take notes on these experiences too, if you want. Definitely, share this easy water spell with others, and recommend it, whenever someone is in need of a healer from a long day. So bless it be!

You are the Fifth Element

You are the last part of the elements, you are ether, and you are spirit
There is nothing you cannot make possible simply because you're near it.
You are the invisibility that reaches beyond the skies above
You are the entity without matter that consists of unity and love.
You are dreams, you are visions; you are destiny and fate
You are in all of the dimensions in which you, harmoniously, pulsate.
When you call the other corners and you end on the pentacle you make,
Just know that you are the force that is the strongest in every breath you take.

Acknowledging the Element of Ether

Spell Work #6

Attempt to be receptive. The element of ether is what divides the empty space between you, as a divine part of its magick, and the heavenly skies and heavens that are above you. Ether is you; you are the center of the pentacle and what makes your part of this puzzle so holy and much needed to be successful and consistent. It is the appreciation of nature that makes your reward your deep involvement with the cosmic connection. You are the bringer of the magick, the vessel the universe has chosen to deliver what needs to be done for not only you, but for all on this planet.

For this spell you might find yourself like a shaman, a Gypsy fortune teller, or a Salem witch, incarnated in your very body. You might feel that you were once burned at the stake, overlooked, misunderstood and left now still starving for answers to why these things have crushed you and are still crushing you.

You will now shadow booth and see your ancestors to familiarize yourself with the miraculous aspects to this element ether, and also the miraculous part of it all, found in you.

Find a room that can be heavily embodied with complete darkness. Not a single trace of sunlight, or any light for that matter, can find a way to seep in through any crack or opening. There must be only black night around your being, to where your eyes cannot even adjust. However, do have only one candle handy. This will be your source of illumination. Have a mirror in front of your face, and the candle somewhere closely below you. Now stare at your own reflection in the mirror. Transcend and foresee your own eyes looking back into you. Stare and gaze until you begin to see your eyes start to transform and your face be replaced with someone else's face that you are sure is not your own. Say these words, yet do not be surprised if you are so locked into the eyes that are looking into you, that you will not be permitted to speak right away. If you are able, recite this. "By the element ether, with my spirit so true, I gaze into this mirror and my ancestors, I call upon you. Reveal your faces before me, in the place of mine. Also reveal to me my future, and what I will see in due time. Answer all questions that I know are buried inside me already known. Then when the light comes back never let me walk this earth alone. So bless it be!"

Now sit there and ask as much as you want or that you can, to the many faces you will see. You will notice that some faces you will recognize and some you will not. Regardless of what you see, you surely will be well aware of the power of this spell and the potential for truth that it holds. That is truly up to what you are ready to ask for. If you can, be this prophet with this element until the sun rises. Then when you are done, snuff your candle, thanking all the ancestors for joining you. Most importantly, while your predictions and visions from this experience are fresh in your mind, document as much as possible in your book of shadows. Reading it later might be very beneficial for you and others. So bless it be!

A Woman's Anthem

This is a poem I dedicate to every lady and little girl
For both the moment they come into and also leave this world
But, not to just any woman do I write this poem for,
But rather to the ones that deserve this and so much more
To the proper girls, the polite ladies, who just always did what was right
The ones who one day decided, instead that they would rather fight
For the chance to be noticed for all the smiles they let just fade
Yet also the courage to be proud of all the mistakes they have made
These words are for those wounded girls, every wild and reckless soul
All you girls that could never seem to be under control
For every girl who decided she was not going to cry
Who ran away, in the dark, and trusted the moon in the sky
The outcasts, the witty ones, the ladies taking on any dare

Dressed in obscene clothes, causing their neighbors to stare
This poem is for all the times that no one understood
For every time you did something no one ever thought you could
You carried an untamed spirit; even still you refuse the social norm
And I am sure you'd rather stand out than ever dare conform
This anthem is written for the lonely girls, with broken hearts still carried
For the widows in black, forced to witness their soulmates be buried
For the women who are prone to enduring all the pain
Who still can talk to angels, and find comfort in the rain
Who carry a look in their piercing eyes that reveals all the truth they have seen
Where life has been all or nothing and never in between
When you feel as though you can't seem to escape another day
You somehow still shine and the hurt begins to sway
With your smudged mascara, and poetry you adapt so well
And with every near-death experience you survived you had another story to tell
For all the ladies that are mothers in this crazy world we're in
To show you all my gratitude, I don't know where to begin

For the mothers who when they were younger, gave their parents grief
Yet saw their own faces staring back at them, in disbelief
Growing up with blood-stained jeans and love letters to your crush
Always being told to say, "Thank you" and yet also being told to hush
You now dare to raise your daughters the way that you wish you would have been
And you do it still with no regrets, and with the will to do it again
This poem goes out to all the elders that taught us about poise
The ones who made sure we never chased the boys
For the ladies that taught us all to sit up straight, and to always be kind
And when we were starving, broken, or ready, could always read our minds
For the home-cooked meals, the stories shared, and the gifts you gave
For the patience yet the discipline when our bad asses would misbehave
For all the women who are now our guardian angels freed from this cruel place
With every step you walked in life you did it with unique grace
This poem recites words romantically about all impacts you made by being true

Each prayer us ladies whisper to ourselves, we know you are hearing too
Women are not always easy, and can be evil and insane
You know we talk shit, we cause scenes and we drink too much champagne
We refuse to be challenged; we forget to return favorite shoes
We are moody, and we are picky, and we often cannot choose
But deep down all of us hold a certain knowing, a linking connection
We understand intuition, nature, and the universe with perfection
So lastly, I would like to write about all the loyal women I have ever known
The ones who wore the label BFF or never let us walk alone
Who put lipstick on our faces, and curled our hair before a date
Who would kill for you, lie for you, and you knew you met because of fate
It's these friendships that women share that no one can touch
And these women who truly have saved our lives so much
So remember your favorite women every time you hear your favorite song
When the dress fits you just right, and when you find the will to be strong

Every time you hold your head up high, and you inspire someone looking down
Just know you have set an example for all women, ready to get up off the ground
So whether you are dropout or homecoming queen
Whether you are on a diet or smoking like a fiend
Every lady from their first Barbie until they take their last breath
Have something in common even if it's all that they have left
It's courage to find the way on these bumpy paths we're forced to take
And it's hard when society has shamed us since we were first burned at the stake
We all have been the goddess, the queen, the slut, the snob, and the 'Whatever they want us to be'
We have read our names on bathroom stalls or carved into our favorite tree
Wherever you find yourself right now, in this world, at the end of the day
Just keep smiling, because deep down, you know you'll always find your way.

Covens and Gatherings

Spell Work #7

Attempt to be open. After the new moon has passed, there will always be a very strong and creative energy in the air. It will linger and allow you to seek out and find new-found friends or reunions with powerful people you have not seen in a while. These are the types of people that teach us the kinds of lessons we keep with us forever, and it is often from another witch. These people are on our paths in our lives as reminders that we are all on the same journey. Well, in unity there is strength and this time of every month will put things into perspective. Embrace the deep and spiritual conversations. Inhale the knowledge and the new-found epiphanies. These are the times when everything just clicks, and discovery is made within and yet made possible from reaching out. There are no coincidences. Your social interactions with people that you share these moments with are so vital not only for you and them, but also for the world. You change this world every day. Maybe it is time in your life to consider the possibility to include a coven or circle to make your magick blossom, with others that share your beliefs, ideas, and trust. This is not a mandatory decision, but it surely is a very awesome option that we all have. It's your craft, so do whatever you feel necessary.

Remember to have fun in these moments, but to also be wise with the people in which you choose to share these moments with. There is no betrayal like one made by someone you thought you had made a spiritual connection with that turned out to be with bad intentions. These are people that you will know in your heart are worth making the effort to love in this magick way. So, if it is not forced, hurried or fake, take the first step and initiate the bond and seal the deal. This can be done in many traditional, religious and modern ways. I have a personal suggestion of how it can be made official. The point of this spell is to seal the deal.

It will convey and confirm that you are all people, making a choice to be witches and to hold your bond sacred. You're announcing that you trust the people around you wholeheartedly, and there will always be a loyalty that comes with the trust you are giving.

The way I find most pleasing is to gather in a circle. Sit comfortably, and set the mood with candles, music and all the other appropriate essentials. Choose an item to represent your authority. This item will be passed around the circle. It can be a wand, a sword, a stone or gem, a talisman, anything you find to be holy. Now pass around the item, and when it is in the hand of the speaker, they will at that time have the opportunity to announce their place in that circle. They will speak about who they are, and what their purpose is in your circle or coven. When they are speaking, all others in the circle will listen, without judgement and with the intention of keeping their words secret whenever the circle is complete. Nothing leaves the environment, or is spoken about again, other than at the next gathering that will come later.

These moments are just beginnings, and there are so many unexpected times to come. This is what makes these powerful circles so amazing. The strength of everyone in the circle, all contributing their own unique qualities and talent, is the purpose for covens. This has never changed and will never cease. We are all together in this world, fighting for the same justices, purity and equality. If you can find the time together to hold hands and recite these words, it will make it set in stone (feel free to use your own words if you like). "We gather together in this circle with power and with love. All that we hold dear comes from below and from above. We will forever honor all that is sacred and true. With the intentions of good, our magick will be pure with all we do. So bless it be!"

These gatherings can be held whenever you feel the time to be. They will be where you get drunk, tell stories, dance, chant, cast spells, and shed laughter and tears. You will make eternal friendships and eternal magick. These are the circles that ignite ideas that change our crazy world. These are the people that become your soul families in this lifetime. Cherish moments that you are blessed to share in these sacred circles, and please write about these experiences and read out loud to your coven. Your words are golden and it is just as relevant to listen as it is to speak. Never stop learning and guiding. Your journey will always take you to places of your wildest dreams. There is no limit to your everlasting voyage. So bless it be!

Existence

Every part of the universe is a work of art.
With every star as it twinkles, with every beating heart,
There's an energy that transfers below and above.
It creates its own magical connection, just like making love.
It's when you stop and listen, and witness all that you embrace,
You realize how involved you are, and how you are needed in this place.
You become humbled by the truth, that all the beauty that you view
Is also returning its admiration of being in awe of you.
The stars are so far in distance, yet so close to your soul.
You are the missing piece that makes everything entirely a whole.
You are also a masterpiece so powerful and complete,
Joining the rhythm of life, by your heart's harmonious beat.
We are only here for a moment, to join this miraculous dance,
Yet in this existence, it is never only just by chance.
When we gain wisdom, and let go of all we doubt,
We are gifted with the evidence of what it is all about.

There is so much you will understand, once you no longer resist.
Then, the possibilities are endless just because you exist.

Casting Your Circle and Calling the Corners

Spell work #8

Attempt to be traditional. You are familiar with the elements earth, air, fire, water and ether. You now understand the directions, characteristics, the seasons, and the signs for each element. Most importantly, you have felt each element in its very essence. You have become connected to each element, and made magick in the process. Now it is time to traditionally put all of the elements together, by casting your circle and calling the corners. This is so sacred and relevant for your spell work.

The whole purpose for casting a circle is creating the space in which your magick is protected, and more powerful. This circle must be closed while in your practice, and then opened when you are complete in your spell casting. There are many ways to lock in the magick into your circle. These ways can take many different tools. Feel free to get creative in how you create your circle. Always remember you can still maintain your traditions while adding your own unique character to your craft. This is always true; these are always spells that come from you, so you are your own creator and your own magician who will be recognized by the deities.

I like to make a circle with large rocks, boulders, or with branches that already fall off of trees that I feel speak to me. You can use sand, salt, stones, or anything you feel is sacred. You can also take a wand and make an imprint in the sand or dirt, or you can paint one, invisibly in the air, shaping a circle. Your finger makes a great starting and ending point to shape a circle. There is no wrong way to do this. Just make sure the space created is large enough around you to do all your magick in.

When you are ready, stand in the north position, and begin to call your corners to find and wake the gods. They will join you. Speak with purpose and gratitude, yet with a force of strength and truth. As you stand facing north speak, "Goddess of the North, for the element earth I call upon you to join me in this circle." Already placed by your feet can be something to represent the element earth. Green candle, dirt or soil, or flowers or seeds, all work well. Then, go to the east and say these words, "Goddess of the East, for the element air, I call upon you to join me in this circle." At your feet, there should be a yellow candle, incense or a feather. Now stand facing the south and say, "Goddess of the South, for the element of fire, I call upon you to join me in this circle." Below you might be a wooden branch or wand or knife or sword. Then, face the west and say, "Goddess of the West, for the element of water,

I call upon you to join me in this circle." At your feet should be seashells, or a chalice of water. Now stand at the center, lighting a white candle as your center, and at your altar say, "I light this candle for the element of ether and spirit; protect this circle and bless this magick." Now light all of the candles, starting with the north, and ending again in the west. Now feel free to say more words if you feel necessary, or not. It is up to you. Carry on with your spell work, until you feel the need to reopen your circle. This permits the energy and you and others to leave this sacred space. Starting from the west, snuff each candle, thanking the gods for their assistance, then walk counterclockwise, starting at the west and ending in the north. Say these words, "Thank you for assisting me in my protection and my magick. I reopen this circle, so bless it be!" Repeat this at every element's corner. Enjoy and write about your many future magick spells and sacred circles. There is much to be done, my sister. So bless it be!

Never Burn Again

I told myself, *"I will never burn again,"* for I can still feel the death
Of lives ago, when I inhaled the heavy smoke, while taking my last breath.
Above my arms tied so tight, as I looked down at the crowd,
I can still hear their screaming in my ears, so hateful and so loud.
    Before they took my life away, I had a dream of smoke.
Frantic then, I jumped out of bed as I began to choke.
    My cauldron bubbling over, my broomstick on the floor,
It was a sign, revealing there would soon be a knock at the door.
    I braided my long raven hair, and held my talisman in my hand.
I watched my hourglass drop its last grain of sand.
    My cat Midnight brought in a white dove and dropped it at my feet.
I used its blood, and dipped my quill, until my spell was complete.

Suddenly, dozens of angry men barged in and dragged me out into the night.
Their jealous wives waited for me, beneath the moon that shined, so bright.
I did not struggle at all, for I already knew the future ahead of me.
They thought they were committing murder, but they were really setting me free.
The stars, the clouds, and the trees, were all witnesses I befriended.

I knew I would be reborn to see them again, as soon as the ceremony ended.
Once it did, one of the men found a folded parchment paper in the field.
He opened it, so astonished at what the smudged words revealed.
My words of blood still wet, and smudged on his fingertips,
He read these words out loud, as if they had been spoken off my lips,
"To all those who have taken the life of an innocent witch tonight,
I curse you to be damned to hell and to suffer in agony and fright,
You do not know the torture that awaits you, from which you can't escape.
This is the karmic law of three, unfolding as my reward and your fate.

You will be eternally damned, but for me death is not the end
I will return, so it shall be, I will never burn again!"

Invoking the Moon Goddess

Spell Work #9

Attempt to be intoxicated. During the full moon, this spell is extremely powerful. It is an invocation. This makes any spell more potent, because you will have the strength of the goddess of the moon, Diana, inside you and with you in spirit. After you draw your circle and call the elemental corners, stand beneath the stars and the bright moon. You may use a wand or power stone, or wear a talisman and your favorite witch's attire. You may also simply use your own hands and fingertips. The point of this ritual is to feel the intoxication of the full moon. This will energize you and empower you, so you might feel a little bit amped, drunk, or dizzy. These are normal and wonderful sensations.

Hold out your hand or wand to where it is pointed at the moon. Cover the moon in your view, and visualize all of its power being sent down on you, through your pointed hands, down your arm, and into your body. Feel Diana's moon warmth, and embrace her magick. Then say these words. "Diana, goddess of the moon so bright, I invoke you tonight. Fill me up with your power, until the coming witching hour. So bless it be!" Then as you finish reciting these words, place your pointed hand over your heart. You will feel this important part of the spell, strongly. Picture all of the moon's magick filling up your heart and then casting a beacon of bright, white light all around your being.

Afterwards, enjoy the time you have this goddess inside you. Cast spells with confidence, and then journal about your amazing experience. So shall it be!

Not so Trendy Witch

I suppose it's in the blood, to have magic pumping through your veins.
When all my energy is depleted, suddenly, I feel the lightning and it rains.
The source is more than around me, it is within my control.
I've done my best to remain pure, keeping good intentions in my soul.
My mother murdered when I was a baby, I believe she left something behind.
For me it was the gift of psychic intuition, to seek and then to find.
Call it a blessing or a curse. It was something I could not change.
And I remember being a child that everyone viewed as strange.
By the time I reached the age of twelve, I was skilled at astrology,
Reading lines on palms, and tarot cards, as my own psychology.
Everyone would come to me for insight, and to tell them what lay ahead
And so my mother's gift, I passed on, to everyone else instead.

Have you ever wished inside yourself? Have you witnessed that wish unravel?

Have you ever seen your own death, or dared to astral travel?

Contacting spirits, casting spells, and seeing auras around everyone I met,

Well, that was the life I've always lived, and I'm not alone I bet!

I have met other natural witches and also witches in denial.

I guess we all resonate with a certain haunting, and unique style.

I have also met the soulless ones that are evil and sly.

Energy vampires, Satians and assholes, that tried to suck me dry.

I have cleansed houses with poltergeists; I've been hexed and possessed,

Okay with my experiences, because it helped me to rise above the rest.

Maybe you can relate, knowing how it feels to trust your inner magic completely?

I have always known who I have always been, but I carried it discretely.

I have seen sceptics transform when I revealed their darkest secrets no one knew.

I have shocked those who didn't believe me, once my warnings to them came true.

But all this time I have been on the wrong path, guiding everyone along the way,

Avoiding the magic that should have been happening in my life today.

I have outgrown the genuine connection that I flowed with in my youth.

I have forgotten what true blessings are really about and lost sight of the truth.

Times have changed so drastically, since I was a child, somehow.

Where witches were seldom seen before, they exist everywhere now.

I am not talking about women who want to learn, grow, and commit.

I am referring to the posers that are not witches, with too much ego to admit

They are not in admiration, dedication, or even any desire to be.

They are liars and they claim a title that is shared with others and with me.

It is the latest fashion, and just an extreme Gothic aftermath.

When I witness these imposters, I don't know if I want to scream or laugh.

While I know that magic is open to anyone who wants to embrace it.

I can't just watch it become misunderstood, and allow myself to face it.

Just yesterday I retired from giving spiritual readings and advice to all.

I will have to just ignore all my spirit guides, and refuse to take their calls.

No exceptions for anyone. The future is no longer even mine to see.

Yet, I cannot escape the witch that lives, embedded inside of me.
 So I will continue struggling to get through the crowds of women in black hats.
I will avoid all of their pentagram jewelry, and their poor abandoned cats.
 I will keep meeting all the walking, living gods fate swings my way.
I will be counting corners in the shadows, like a child at play.
 So take advice from someone who has seen things that you cannot conceive.
Trust me you don't really want this package, unless you truly believe.
 All of the enlightened ones, from every culture and every race
Will join forces and one day rule this world, and make it such a magical place.
I also witness love evolving, from every stranger to every friend.
And to me, that is so much more amazing, than any kind of witchy trend!

Cleansing and Protecting

Spell Work #9

Attempt to be protective. From time to time a witch such as yourself is surely needed when it comes to being a ghost hunter. It is in your blood to sense energies and even spirits in the areas and environments in which you find yourself present. This is in your roots, to be Buffy, slaying vampires and demons in your own unique ways. So in this spell work you will learn a formal way that has worked traditionally for centuries. This is especially in the cases of protecting what rightfully belongs to you or someone else in need of your help, and for cleansing something new to you or that has been tainted and saturated in an energy other than which you desire it to be.

PART ONE

So first let's start off with cleansing a house. This can be in extreme cases or even the slightest of unsettling vibes existing within it. The materials you will need for this cleansing ritual are white sage, matches or a lighter, any preferable power stones worn or left in the place of the desired energy cleansed area, dragon's blood incense if desired, and sea salt if desired. The salt is to be sprinkled in the front doorway to the home. The incense is lit and left to smoke at the east; this is the best place for its potency. It is also best before you begin to call upon or invoke any deities or angels to assist you, depending on how powerful the energies are and what your intuition tells you is necessary.

To begin, breathe deeply, center yourself, be focused, and then do a walk around the area you are cleansing, especially if it is a new environment you have never been to. Now, in my humble experiences there are usually two things I like to skim and scan looking for right away. It is to give me a little bit of preparation for what I am dealing with. I look for the heart of the house and the portal of the house. The heart of the house is detected by the closest feeling of warmth and safety possible to dwell in, within the house and its contents. I have always known right away where this place is found. It will give me a certain sense of comfort and it will be like a magnet pulling me towards it. Clues to the heart of a house are the fact that it is usually where the people living in it tend to be most. It is usually found in the owners' bedroom, but it really can be anywhere in the home. Use your witches' instinct like a metal detector for these things. Once you feel the safety after walking through the home thoroughly, this heart will be where you call upon your guides and begin to light your sage.

Light the sage here, and if you have not already found it, as you begin cleansing, keep searching for the portal. The portal of the house will give you the opposite emotions and you will feel an intense throbbing of anxiety in your solar plexus. You might even feel agitation or a physical discomfort such as weakness or a headache. The portal of a home is where often times, the negative energies or unwanted spirits enter or manifest. This is typically found in attics, bedroom closets, basements, and even beneath stairs. It can be like the heart again, being anywhere in the home. This is true especially if it is a particular hot spot, or an area where death or torture might have occurred in the past. Use your third eye and your sixth sense as a tool to pick up on any visions, sounds, sensations and clues at this time. Do not disregard anything that enters your psychic being, and do not hold back on your receptivity. Remember you are just the vessel and the messenger, so it is never your job to judge anything that you receive. If it does not make sense to you, it might for someone else.

As you seek out the portal, you must also begin the major purpose and duty of this spell. You must cover every area of the home with the smoke of your sacred sage, saying these words. "In the power of earth, air, fire, water and ether, I cleanse this place of all unwanted energies and I protect this place." Feel free to speak other words if you feel they need to be heard. Sometimes you might even feel the need to be stern in your tone or even shout. The key is to never feel intimidated or let on that you are anything other than completely in charge of the place you are cleansing. Remember to cover every window, every doorway, every closet door, hallway, the premises of the back and front yards, the garages, and bathrooms. Keep repeating the words, and cover every space. In the process when you come across your portal, focus immense energy on this area, saying the words with extreme conviction. You might feel the need to surround yourself with an aura of protective light. If you ever feel challenged, say these words, "You have no power over me; as I will it, so shall it be!"

Sometimes, you might find that instead of a portal, it might be a particular item that has held the energy and brought its negativity with it from outside the home, into it. You will know it if this is the case. You should always remove this item. Do not throw it away; keep it, or bury it. Always burn it and let the smoke rise it back to the universe with trust.

After you are complete, use the ashes from your sage and smudge a pentacle in front of the front doorstep. Sprinkle any incense ashes at the doorway. Then, shake off the energy from your work, by flicking invisible water off of your hands, as if shaking your hands dry. Then say, "This house is clean, so bless it be!" Sometimes you might find that certain places might need a few visits because it could also be people re-entering the home that bring the negative energies. If this is the case, try to pinpoint the people and cleanse them with sage, then redo the home as needed. It is also best to shower afterwards with the water spell mentioned earlier in this book.

PART TWO

Now, cleansing can come in handy for other purposes as well. It becomes what might bond or seal a deal between a witch and her powerful divination tools or accessories. The greatest cleansing tools are provided by Mother Nature and the universe here for us already. The most powerful tool of all is the sacred Moon herself. For example, if you receive a crystal ball or deck of tarot cards, simply leaving them to be christened by the cleansing and the powers of the moon all night, especially when it is new or full, can be highly effective. It will make your new items officially yours and yours alone. All of your new and old witches' tools that are especially powerful and sacred to you can be whenever deemed necessary re-cleansed. This will make your items purified and always clean both spiritually and emotionally.

Another handy, natural tool is salt, especially sea salt or from the ocean. Letting a crystal or stone, or anything that will fit in a bowl, simmer and bathe in sea salt makes it pure and back to its origin and roots. Water also can cleanse not only the item but the body. This works as well with smoke that rises and the sun rays that shine upon us.

My best advice to you, my dear witch, is to never underestimate the power of nature and how much of the tools provided for anything are always within your reach. Keep not only your items and your rituals pure, but mainly your intentions. So bless it be!

A Gift and It's in the Blood

It's in the blood I hold so well
That I bleed out and that I expel.
I may have for years learned to dread
I became scared every time I bled.

I viewed it as an unholy thing
I knew each time magick it could bring.
Yet, despite being aligned with the orbital moon
Mother Nature's monthly always arrived too soon.

Yet, it's in the blood that makes me strong
It drips and bleeds for one week heavy and long.
It was once during the full moon and now the new
I have discovered there's much magick to do.

For, it's in the blood that I carry my power.
So many vampires wish to devour.
Gift from the ancestors of my family tree
From the many witches who came before me.

It's in the blood that makes me pure
It soaks and cleanses all that I endure
It realigns my external well-being
It connects me to my future foreseeing.

It's in blood magick that proves my youth
I can still bear children and its living proof.
I am still the maiden, fresh and not yet old
It keeps me confident and keeps my spells bold.

It's in the blood, sex magick is made
It leaves marks and stains that will never fade.
It's always when it's painful, you know you will survive
It's in my blood that has taught me how I am truly alive!

Blood and Sex Magick

Spell Work #10

Attempt to be savage. Despite how many years society has programmed us to hide this natural thing, a woman's menstruation is her strongest power and thickest potion. A true witch can always sense the powers of gravity, and is in cycle with the moon phases with her own period phases. Usually, it is in the new moon and the full moon that a witch finds her period. This is the way of gravity and realignment; call it a curse, but it surely is a blessing when it comes to blood and sex magick.

First of all, one of all the oldest spells in history is done with a drop of menstrual blood in one's drink. It is said to make the drinker in love with the woman whose blood was dropped. Take caution and consideration into doing this spell. Remember the karmic law and take one's own free will into consideration.

There are spells that can be done between lovers in the act of love-making during this potent time of orbital power. To concentrate on one's desire upon climax, while making love during the full moon, is very powerful and almost a hundred percent certain magick.

My advice is to do this spell with one's soulmate and share the same desire. Keep focus, despite the immense pleasure and the many distractions that can take place. To do this act in nature, beneath the moon, after casting your circle and being protected by the elements can make a memorable and passionate experience.

The key is to find comfortability with one's self, especially one's own body. Remember my love, you are the divine feminine, and the power of your blood has been used for ceremonial purposes for centuries. It is only your spell and your blood, so make this act as personal and creative as you like. Remember to journal in your book of shadows for the next witch to read about and learn from your magick. So bless it be!

Shadow

Hey Shadow, of thy lower self I hear you loud and clear
Even though I have prayed that you would disappear
You are going to treat my spirit like a ghost, you will keep haunting
Until I give in and give you all the attention you have been wanting
There's no need to throw a fit, I know that you exist
And I know you will only manifest louder the more that I resist
I have to accept that I can't be perfect, some flaws will not dissolve
But I can at least be stronger and I can grow, learn and evolve
So today I will place my focus on you, my Shadow that is hurting
I will allow myself to feel all the aching, pain that I have been deserting
Even though I may feel embarrassment, shameful, or afraid
I will be true to myself with honesty and it will help the festering to fade

I love you, Shadow, I know that a part of you is being set free.
And I know you have taught me the greatest lesson, to also love me.

Shadow Work

Spell Work #11

Attempt to dig deep. Shadow work is the most needed magick, and also the most difficult. It takes a brave witch to do shadow work. The rewards that come along with this process are limitless.

Let me explain what your shadow is, my sister, and then it's up to you if you are ready to do this type of magick. You will know in your gut and in your heart when the time is right and when you are prepared enough on your path to set out on this journey.

The soul has three parts that are united from within. These are the *lower self,* The *middle self* and the *higher self.* These are all so important and make up who you are: mind, body, and spirit. The following are the definitions of each and the importance in their distinction:

The *lower self* is the part of us that is connected with innocence and the purest aspects of what we came into this world knowing from our last lives. It is childlike, connected to nature and speaks to both other children and to animals. It is our own inner child, and yet also our ability to be connected to the elementals and to the entities in other dimensions. What also makes the *lower self* so important is that this is where the *shadow self* is found. Now the *shadow self* can be more destructive if it is not acknowledged and brought to the surface of reality from time to time. It is like a kid throwing a tantrum if they don't get their way. However, this tantrum is much more severe than a few tears and shouting. This avoidance of the shadow can manifest in our lifestyles. You see, the shadow is every part of us that we avoid and ignore because it is what we fear deep inside ourselves. It is all the flaws, the imperfections and the mistakes that cause us shame. It is our fears of not being perfect or holding up to the standards that either were set by someone else or that we set for ourselves. Obviously, no one is perfect, but that is easier said than done to admit to our egos. The shadow reminds us of this reality, if we allow it to. If we do not, we can form addictions and low self-worth, we can place blame on others, become abused or abusive, and all the other things that can be destructive to our psyches and to who we are as individuals. This is why shadow work is so important for our spiritual growth. Later in this section, I will show you a very productive spell to do shadow work and to do it emotionally and spiritually, and successfully.

The *middle self* is the middle parts of our soul's alignment. This part of us is so needed when it comes to functioning on planet Earth and in a functional way for society and even for being human in this time we are all co-existing. This part of us is what unites and translates between the *lower self* and the *higher self*. It takes care of all the tasks that are made with the physical mind in this tangible world. It stays on top of anything that is needed to be spiritually beneficial to ourselves and to others we meet in need of our assistance. While our source might be the *higher self,* our instinct come from the *lower self,* it's our *middle self* that is the spiritual healer able to flip the cards, toss the stones and gaze into the crystal ball to deliver the divination needed for verbal power and conviction. The *middle self* does acts of justice, activism and holds the meetings and the gatherings for her sisters. The *middle self* is what gets things done, and holds a sense of sincerity and purpose in this world, in this dimension, in this body with soul and with heart, but mainly with an open and focused mind. This is done with respect from others and from the society that is known to have the possibility to judge and not accept anything done. This does not matter; the *middle self* understands the importance of pursuing acts that will bring change just as strongly as the *lower* and *higher selves* do. This part just does it in a more methodical and logical way, in order to make things that are felt with purpose come to life and be manifested.

The *higher self* is the part of us that is connected directly to source. It is where we receive our unseen messages of prophecy, and where we are able to tap into the truth in what the element ether gifts us all the power to connect with. The *higher self* understands and knows all, when it comes to what is best for your soul and your place in this world, in this life and the next. The *higher self* holds every answer to every question when it involves your evolution. Just think of this part as being the excelled and the advanced part of your soul's journey. This is true for every life you have lived and will live, and when you reach your highest level of advancement to being your own goddess and teacher. This is where your visions come in, your dreams from your ancestors and the old crone inside of all of us, who knows all that is needed to prevail over any of the obstacles that could ever stand in your way. This part of your soul is connected to your third eye chakra, and holds the keys to all of the secrets you spend a lifetime learning on your own. It is how we meditate, slay the ego, and become artists. In every song we sing, picture we paint, poem we write, dance we flow in, and magick spell we cast with passion, it is the *higher self* that has guided our beings into creating something beautiful and powerful.

Alignment of Self

To be in alignment with all three parts of your self is difficult but surely possible and necessary in order to be genuinely happy with one's own place in this world. This is where true work can be done to save this place and make our marks as the witches we were born to be. It is especially needed to find our calling and destiny in this life. In order to be fully aligned and happy, shadow work is needed and done to accept that we are perfect in our own imperfections, and it's the flaws that make us human, but the growth in which we wish to change that makes us content with who we are inside.

Shadow Work Meditation

Whenever you feel that it is time, or you might notice yourself acting out in ways that seem out of character for your personality, find a quiet and undisturbed place to heal. Close your eyes and center yourself, focusing on your breathing. As you inhale, think of an emotion about yourself that you block out. This can be an emotion that causes one or repeated mistakes in your life. It can also be insecurity, or something that you feel to be a flaw in your personality. This emotion can be current or in your past. It can be one or more traits, actions, or repercussions. It must be something that you tuck away. The harder it is for you to think about the emotion, the more powerful the healing process will be once it is acknowledged. This can be shame, guilt, fear, lack of confidence, an addiction, jealousy, being too passive, being too aggressive, an act you view as sinful from your conditioning or upbringing, or anything else that you usually dismiss whenever it enters into your mind or spirit. Now, with every exhale focus on where on your body this or these emotions resonate. Where do you feel the feeling on your physical body? Is it heavy on your heart? Do you hold it on your shoulders? Does it give you anxiety that you can feel throb in your solar plexus? Now, as difficult as it might be at first, attempt to focus your thoughts and breaths, particularly on the specific area in your body that you feel the emotion. Give all of your attention to it, and for a moment, sit and linger in this feeling. Just know that it is okay to feel this feeling. It is a wound or discomfort that once recognized and acknowledged, will become a healer in your actions and how you have been negatively acting out. Just remain as calm as possible, keep breathing, and keep feeling the emotion.

Now, try to focus your inhales and exhales on releasing this emotion. Feel an aura of protecting, healing, purple illumination, swelling the part of your body where you felt the emotion. If you feel it is necessary, say these words, or words of your own that feel right. "I am here and I am whole. I accept this emotion of _____, and I allow myself to acknowledge what I have been avoiding. I am safe knowing that my *lower self* and my *shadow self* are in need of healing and I love myself for all that I am. So bless it be." Now visualize that purple healing light getting bigger and filling your entire body. Visualize and accept this light forming its circle from within you to all around you. Feel its sweet protection fill you up and cover you up. It will be there in that circle that you must find your peace. Allow yourself to let go of the mistakes you have made that cannot be changed, in the past. Allow yourself to learn and grow and evolve in the knowing that there are many things that you can change in the present. Let this give you a sense of hope and trust in what the future holds for you on your journey.

Shadow work can take practice, and I cannot promise that it will get easier every time it is revisited. What I can promise is the results you will surely see transform your life, every time you attempt this process. For your strength, priestess, you will surely be rewarded by your shadow and from the universe. This is where true acceptance becomes not only beauty, but pure magick. Good luck on this and remember to write about your bravery in your book of shadows. This spell should be recognized by yourself further down the road upon reflection, and if you want by others who too are ready to take this step to heal their wounded hearts. So bless it be.

A Witch Will Get Ya Back

Some of them are quiet, hiding in the crowd.
Some of them outspoken, and saying their thoughts out loud.
The words are not what matter. It's the intent behind their pack.
If you hurt a witch, I promise a witch will get ya back.

You can call it *hocus pocus*, and try not to feed into the fire.
You can attempt to use your mind, to reject what they desire.
You can try to say "I'm sorry," but if its sincerity you lack,
The apologies will not save you and a witch will get ya back.

Some witches don't want to hurt others, and they try to stop the wrath.
They do their best to try to warn you of the aftermath.
They may even fear their own power, but the universe is intact,
And if you screw them over a witch will get ya back.

Witches truly are just keepers of the truth and that is rarely shown,

And they can be the most honorable souls you've ever known.
So my advice is to be decent, and their power will not attack.
Be good to a witch and then a witch will be good back.

Candle Magick

Spell Work #12

Attempt to trust. Candle magick is the most traditional and yet the most personal type of magick a witch can do. It is a form of meditation and manifestation. Each color candle represents a different intention or area of magick. However, a witch can always utilize her candles to her own unique designs and masterpieces. Candles can be dressed and anointed with different oils for different purposes. They can be carved into with specific symbols and shapes, and they can even be made from scratch using waxes and other additions to their forms. (Example: rose petals, stones, glitter, seashells, etc.) Afterwards, the wax that remains can be kept somewhere safe or carried around with someone, depending on the intent. Again, your most powerful spell will be one you mold and shape from your own artistic touch.

The following are color genres for candles:

Red: For the element of fire, and the south position. For Aries, Leo, or Sagittarius sun signs. It is great for spells involving strength, passion, lust and confidence.

Orange: Great for energy and for vitality.

Blue: For the element of water, and the direction of the west. Used for the signs of Cancer, Scorpio and Pisces. This color candle is great for emotional and harmonious balance. Spells to recharge and revitalize also work well with blue.

Green: This color can be used for money and prosperity spells. Green is also for centering and grounding. It is always used for representing the element of earth and the north direction. It also corresponds with the signs Taurus, Virgo and Capricorn.

Yellow: This color is represented with the element of air and the direction of the east. Also, this color is for the signs Gemini, Libra and Aquarius. Yellow is also used with intellectual spells working with focus and intelligent thinking. It works well with memory and concentration and also our inner child.

Gold: Gold is used for prosperity and abundance and also spirit guide connection. It can be used in the place of the masculine position on your Altar.

Silver: This color is good with astral projection and astral travel, connecting the soul to the body. It can also represent the feminine aspect at your altar.

Pink: This color is for deep and pure love. It is great for romance and manifesting your soulmate.

White: This color is great for cleansing spells and for angel work. It represents the element of ether and is linked to our divine spirit. It is a great color to use as the center of your altar, magnetically attracting the powers of the moon and the deities directly to the center of your circle.

Black: This color is great for black magick, binding, hexing and protection spells. It is a source of banishment and force when needed.

Purple: This is the color that is the most powerful when working with divination and psychic intuition. It helps us to work more in tune with the universe and is connected to the third eye. It is wonderful when working with healing spells. It also an ideal candle color for using tarot, crystal gazing, channeling spirits and ancestors and dowsing.

Candle Manifestation Spell

This spell works well when demanding the universe give you what you desire in your life. As always, choose wisely in what you are asking to be granted. Remember, everything you could ever want is out there waiting to be given to you; you just have to know the correct ways to manifest and truly believe that you will receive your most successful outcome.

Choose a color candle that corresponds to your desire. Light the candle after drawing your circle and calling upon the elements for assistance and protection. As you use your chosen colored candle, light it in front of you at your center. Focus on the flame it creates. Focus on your desire as you gaze into the candle and its power. Snuff the candle; watch the smoke rise up to the universe, carrying your desire with it. Do this for seven days, preferably beneath the new moon. You should surely see your results begin to manifest by the time the full moon approaches. To make it even more potent in its results, keep the wax from the spell somewhere safe until the full moon, and then spread the wax anywhere you like. (Within your drawn circle, at your feet, at your doorstep, anywhere you like.)

You might choose to say these words each day as you gaze if you feel necessary. "I light this candle of magick fire, to bring forth that which I desire. All my intentions true with every part of me, as I will it so shall it be!"

Remember to write about your experiences, feelings, and results from this manifestation. It will bring you confirmation that your spell is working and that will bring you even more confidence in your spell casting. So bless it be!

The Day of the Dead

Just for tonight, this year I wait for your arrival
I am very grateful as I linger in my blessed survival.

You did not make it alive, like I am lucky to be
Yet, tonight your spirit is permitted to walk this earth like me.

I have nothing to fear, I am only so excited to feel your presence
I know the way it will be the moment I can feel your essence.

For, I have missed you my beloved, more than you know
But tonight I will be able to let these feelings go.

I have set up an altar in your memory, just how you would have done
I have cooked a meal for you and I am offering you some.

So sit with me and join this elegant dinner that is honoring you
And I will be so happy just to be next to the spirit I once knew.

I know you have been expecting this day to come for the dead
I am sad that for you no more living days lie ahead.

But just once a year, at least we have our chance to sit together at peace
And then I have to let you go back to join the deceased.

So let's play your favorite songs; let's smile about memories we share
Let me pay attention to the signs you show me that will swarm me everywhere.

Let me shed a tear if it feels like falling, let me wipe it with pride
And I will enjoy every moment that I have you tonight at my side.

I love you, my long-lost soul, I always have I always will.
The lessons you have taught me, you are teaching me still.

From you I am learning about sorrow, gratitude, and living with you gone
And most importantly you have taught me that without you, life goes on.

So for what it's worth I am proud that Halloween is here tonight
And although I will be sad, I will say farewell with the morning light.

I will miss you until next year, I am sure you'll hear my cries
Mainly, you've taught me how the body is temporary, yet the spirit never dies.

Honoring the Deceased on Halloween

Spell Work #13

Attempt to channel spirits. Hallows Eve is the one night of the year that the dead rise. All of our loved ones, ancestors, and anyone who has touched us that has passed on is honored on this lovely holiday. It is a witch's favorite time of year, because by nature we have learned to understand death so well. We know that death is rebirth and part of the universal law for cycle and transition to occur. All death must never be feared or viewed as spooky, because it is true reality that one day we too, will share the experience of our own death. It is in these eerie and witchy nights that we acknowledge the spirits and the ghosts at play in the shadows. We are to welcome this trusted energy, and allow it to bring us comfort and peace. It will be Halloween, with this ritual, that you will find the most beneficial remedy to your longing heart and your mourning soul, my dear witch. It is okay to utilize this day as a time to place all of your attention on one or more of your deceased loved ones. It is okay to acknowledge them for today, because even though they are gone, they have left their mark in this world and on who we are. So feel whatever you must feel, and do not hold back on what you wish to realize in these moments. They might hurt or bring joy; all emotion felt is okay. Just journal in your magick book, and release all of your suppression and your memories of it all in your fluid and sentimental words. There truly is no better magick than your own poetry or words of wisdom, written in these dark and lonely times of grieving.

Ritual to Honor Your Lost Love
Part One: Decorating your Altar

If I have ever explained a more important time to take care and thorough love with your altar it is now. Although your altar will change often as you might change it with your moods, your spells, and the seasons, this altar is for the one you have lost that will be visiting you the night of October 31st.

Before the sun goes down, it is best to be prepared for the arrival of your lost love. You will be having a dinner with them as the guest of honor. You may have anyone there at your dinner party, just remember not to invite anyone who you would not have at any regular dinner party to this one. That is true for the living and the spirits that you are considering. So with that being in mind, place your thoughts on who it is you will be honoring at dinner time. Maybe it is someone you just recently lost; maybe someone you have been missing for a long time; maybe someone you have never met but know exists in your bloodline, or maybe a few souls that you feel should join you. All of these are good dinner guests for your evening. Once you make that decision, you must begin to decorate your altar accordingly.

Think of all the things that your dearly departed found to be favorable. What were their favorite things, what reminds you of them, what colors did they love, what favorite meal, favorite songs, most flattering and cherished pictures and sentimental treasures? Decorate your altar the way they would have done, and do it with patience, care, and a lot of thought. You and your ghostly soul to come – both will appreciate every part of it. Get creative. Maybe there is a piece of jewelry they wore that you would like to decorate your altar candle with? Maybe you have their ashes or their letters? Just place these items beautifully beside the elemental candles of your corners and within your sacred space of a circle drawn with love.

Begin cooking their favorite dinner dish now, and then set the table. Feel free to have a soft musical background, playing a song that reminds you instantly of them, whenever it is heard. You will begin to feel their spirit present as they anticipate the moment the meal is ready to be served. Pay attention to the subtle signs as confirmation that they are near you. You will know exactly what speaks to you in this moment.

Part Two: Dinner with Your Lost Loved One

Now serve the meal to everyone joining you in spirit as well as in the flesh. Now, while some dinner parties are meant for celebration, and talkative interactions, and mingling, this dinner is sacred in its silence. This is when you spend your dinner date listening, observing, and remembering the deceased guest of honor. Feel free to cry silently or laugh a little if the opportunity presents itself. Just whatever you might find yourself doing, at least make the time to share the beautiful silence; this is so important and it is for their respect and devotion that you do this. This is how any things they wish to express to you are definitely heard. Busyness and loud distractions of everyday life can make it very hard to receive messages from our lost loved ones, but tonight is their night and we will listen in humility and love.

After you have shared a peaceful time and meal together, when the time feels right, say these words as if you are making a toast. "Ancestors, lost and missed souls that are with me tonight, I thank you and I honor you with these flames I ignite. By the power of all you have done for me, you are remembered tonight, so bless it be!" Now light your candles, starting from the north earth and so on, clockwise; when you come to your ether center altar candle, say these words. "I light this candle in the element ether and for the spirit of my departed; our time together on Halloween has started. May you join me until the sun rises at dawn, and once you leave, may your memory always live on. So bless it be!"

Now spend the rest of your night however you wish. Dance around a fire, cast spells, tell stories, get drunk, cry, laugh and play. Your lost loved one will be with you in spirit and near you in this dimension. So will many other lost loved ones. The night will be potent and full of thick energies of the unknown. Do not be afraid, for this is the beauty of this holy night. The things we might not always see are at times what protect us the most. Never be afraid of what lurks in the shadows of this night, for it will be everything you have been missing and longing to be with since you experienced your first loss. They are near on this night, and they will always be in your hearts forever more. So bless it be!

It's Up to Us Now

It's up to you whether or not you find me, alone just like you are.
It's up to me whether or not I find myself to also heal from every scar.
These wounds we both have gotten, from the reckless paths we choose
Are how we both find comfort and how we both know we can't lose.

For when we find each other, and accept how much we are alike
Nothing can stand a chance, so any danger can go ahead and take a strike.
There's just some things that we can handle that others never could
And we can take the pain gladly, and with only intentions of the greater good.

You can look into my eyes, and strangely read my mind
I can sense your emotions so when you wander, I am never too far behind.
We both would rather be lost, unknowing, than found in the same place

And we will keep on going, leaving footsteps we hope
 the wind will soon erase.

This world is sinking quickly; all we love on this planet
 is drowning fast
The future's destiny can be discovered in the repeated,
 historic past
Just like witches before us have suffered, they will
 suffer once we are gone
But if we fail to come together when it matters, there is
 no reason to live on.

Yet you and I both know we are all too proud to give in
We understand that for everything that is ending,
 something is ready to begin.
You will be at my side, and we will prevail, some way,
 somehow.
But first the choice is up to us to take this risk; it's up to
 us now.

It's up to us now, for the justice and the rite to be free
We will choose to save all we can, as we will it, so shall
 it be!
It's up to us now; it's up to you and me
Challenge us if you dare! And so it is, and bless it be!

17 Second Manifestation

Spell Work #14

Attempt to be imaginary. This spell is so powerful, and I used it as a healing spell to save my life. It did, it truly did. This spell can be used as any wish that you want to fulfill that you feel the universe can give you. Again, remember to believe in your wish with the heart of a child and the conviction of an alchemist. Remember to always choose your wish wisely, as I know you will. Enjoy and please again, if you feel the urge, journal on the powers of this one. You are going to see immediate results with this manifestation. Please share it with others who too are in need of a little magick and wish-fulfilment in their lives.

To begin, meditate or center yourself in any way that you are comfortable, and make sure you are in an undisturbed place that is quiet and peaceful. You must remain focused to ensure you are thorough in this spell. The good news is it is a very short time you will need this solitude. Actually only seventeen seconds. Seventeen seconds is worth a lifetime in cosmic and universal time in the realm of the ether. It is worth a century's amount of time, and it is plenty of time to get your wish fulfilled.

Now think of an item or object that you love, but have no emotional attachment to. For example, I chose feathers. So you can use anything like symbols of stars, moons, roses, snowflakes, whatever you feel connected to but not attached to. Now, think of your wish and lock it into your chosen item or object. Connect the two things together. Now hold onto your wish and your object in your heart and your third eye for seventeen seconds. Really focus all of your power, will, and trust on this seventeen seconds. When you are done, you might feel the need to say, "So bless it be!" You do not have to say anything. Just watch the immediate results.

When I say results, I mean results that will definitely surprise you and bring you great joy. When I did this spell, I began to see feathers everywhere. It was so crazy! I found a feather from a hawk in the middle of a casino, immediately after I did my manifestation. My son brought me home hummingbird feathers that he found walking home from school. I acquired feathers from everywhere at least once a day. I had so many of them I began to make dreamcatchers out of them. The beauty of all of this is, the more items you find that you chose connected to your wish, the more it is a confirmation that your wish is closer to coming true. It is your evidence that your manifestation is in motion.

You will know when your spell is over and when it is final. I know for me I healed myself and I was better, and people ask me how I got well. I simply say,

"Feathers." I still mean that wholeheartedly. So will you. So bless it be.

Ask Yourself Witch, Have You Made Your Mark?

Ask yourself, witch, "Have you made your mark?"
Did you do all you could to ignite your inner spark?
At the end of the day, before you close your eyes to rest,
Can you dream, knowing nothing weighs on your chest?

Ask yourself, goddess, if tomorrow you never wake,
Could you say that you took all the risks you could take?
Did you live yesterday with all the life that you had?
Or would you reincarnate again feeling so sad?

Ask yourself, my sister, "Did you always follow your heart?"
Have you helped this Earth by doing your part?
Have you refused to falter or turn the other cheek?
Were you a strong example to others when they felt weak?

Ask yourself, shaman, "Did you heal others in your path?"
Did you heal yourself in the process, or settle with wrath?
Did you open your mind; did you trust your sixth sense?

When the whole world was too quiet, did you make it intense?

Ask yourself, priestess, "Have you shown the world your power?"
Did you know how to utilize the moments of the witching hour?
Did you cast spells that were created by the artist in you?
And, most importantly, did you keep your intentions true?

Ask yourself, maiden, "Did you voyage out to the unknown?"
Did you ever set out on your journey completely alone?
Did you trust that you would arrive at your destination okay?
Leaving your bare footprints as a map, leading the way?

Ask yourself, mother, "Have you discovered your worth?"
Have you realized that you have a purpose on this Earth?
Did you listen to those who also share the divine spark?
Who have also questioned if they truly made their mark?

Final Thoughts

Your Everlasting Spell Work

Attempt to continue evolving. Just like the cycle of the moon, the seasons, and life and death, you, my goddess, will continue evolving and going through many cycles throughout your life. You might find, especially through journaling and looking back on what you have written, that one year you might be into only solitary work, and then the following year be into covens with others. This is okay. It is always best to never know everything. As well as being an impossibility, knowing everything would prevent the possibility of continuous growth and knowledge. As much joy as it is to discover new wisdom in your craft, and obtain new perspectives from the opinions of others, the most powerful magick is the lessons that we learn for ourselves along the path of our journey. To witness our magick be born, and then after it is crafted, to witness it blossom and truly work, is a beautiful feeling of confidence in our art. We all are searching for the sense of belief in ourselves, and it is truly found with the passion, love and faith that we have in everything we create. Now we must remind ourselves to constantly take this magick a bit further. We must do it for the greater good, for the cause, and most importantly to shape others and this world we live in together.

So now, as I close this chapter and this poetry spell book, I have to ask you to ask yourself if you are doing all you can in this moment in your life to contribute. I mean in all of the ways and forms that you feel in your gut and in your heart that you are pulled towards, are you following these aspects or blocking them out? I know how easy it is to just move forward and to ignore the ways that magick and nature and even society might call us. Life can be full of distractions, and these distractions keep us from fulfilling the magick we are born to do. So we must find a way to make time, remind ourselves, and believe in ourselves enough to do what we feel is our part, and what we feel is the magnet of our own destinies. Where we are pulled to, who knows? The beauty is in the mystery and the unknown, unseen forces that come with it all. That's what makes us witches similar. This purpose keeps us all connected. We are supposed to change whatever we feel is necessary and within our power to change, especially ourselves.

So at the end of the day, are you happy with your magick and your addition to this beautiful craft? Is there something that you feel is wrong or unjust that you can change? Do you have the power to alter the course that these unfair circumstances are on? Is there a creative process that you have felt in your bones and have been dying to explore? Are you still putting off the desires that need fulfilling? Are you doubting your creative ideas, and excusing the birth of your ideas for not having enough time? Well, now is the time. It is for this reason that you must make time. The universe needs you. I promise you in all your pain, your stress, and your experiences, there is something just dying to be born. All of your hardships can be transformed. All of your inner, creative magick is inside of you. There are creations, artistically dying to be created, that only you can create. I promise you, it will change the lives of others, and it will change who you are as a person in the process. This is what our evolution is all about, and it is an amazing gift that we are blessed to share.

So do something today, and make it count. Cast a spell that you know will assist in the making of something that is beyond being needed and is actually essential for this world. Never doubt the power you possess and the magick that you can make. This is all that I humbly ask that you remember and take with you, after reading this book.

So please write poetry of your own, create spells from the depths of your soul, and find others who will share this gift with you. It is the strength that we all carry in our spirits that will set the examples for others. What we have learned, from our mothers and grandmothers, is what we will leave behind to teach our children and grandchildren. They are just as powerful as we are, and share the same love for this Earth, I promise you. So in unity there is strength, and the magick is inside of you. I know you will take pride in everything you create. There is no reward as sacred as the sense of completion and wholeness that links you with the universe; especially after you have created the manifestation all on your own. There is much magick to be made, and there's no time like the present. So what are you waiting for? I am with you every step of the way, like I know you are for me in return.

"My dear sister, your hand in mine; walk with me in this important time.

Be confident, be brave, and be kind. On this journey, love we shall find. So bless it be."

Spell Dictionary, Keywords and Appendix

Useful Little Tool

Legendary Spell casters
Aleister Crowley
King Solomon
Merlin

Supplies
Books:
'To Ride a Silver Broomstick: New Generation Witchcraft' by Silver RavenWolf
'True Magick: A Beginner's Guide' by Amber K
'A Witches' Bible: The Complete Witches' Handbook' by Janet Farrar, Stewart Farrar
'Buckland's Complete Book of Witchcraft' by Raymond Buckland
'The Element Encyclopedia of 5000 Spells' by Judika Illes

Oils
Dragon's blood
Planetary oils
Astrological signs
Jasmine
Lavender
Peppermint
Lemon
Ginger
Herbs and plants and Nature's essentials
Belladonna
Hemlock
Mugwort

Ginger
Sea salt
Rain water
Holy water
Rice
Menstrual blood
Cemetery dirt
Dragons or doves
Blood ink
Feathered quills
Charcoal
Sandalwood
White sage
Silver
Thyme
Personal power stones and jewelry (all items worn for magick should be charged under the full moon for intensified energy)
Rings with powerful stones (preferably silver and/or poison rings)
Charms (different stones and symbols for different intentions)
Talismans
Amulets
Dowsing pendulums (Any personal favorite item of jewelry that makes you feel the most confident and brings you the most luck)
Altar supplies
Beeswax candles (one silver, one gold, or green, blue, red and yellow for the elements)
An altar candle centered and white
Choice of incense
Pentacle
Brass bell
Asthame
Cauldron
Staff or wand

Optional items for your altar, of your preference:
Crystals
Crystal ball
Essential oils

Dragon's blood
Mirrors
Wine
Items that have been charged with energy and that hold magical or sentimental significance to you, etc.

Witch's 'must haves'
Witch's cupboard
Broomstick
Cauldron
Candles (many colors for different desires)
Incense (variety of types for different purposes)
Attire (hats, make-up, boots, goddess dresses, masks, headpieces, gloves, capes, lingerie, nets and stockings)
Silver cord
Red wine
Book of shadows (journal of spells)
Wand (homemade or bought)
Snuffer
Scrying bowls
Crystal balls
Runes
Tarot cards
Potion bottles
Dragon's blood
Dragon's blood ink
Magick mirrors
Candle holders (preferably brass or silver)
Altar space
Larger stones for casting circles
Powders and magick dusts
And last but not least, a black cat.

The Many Ways to Practice Magick
Voodoo
Wiccan
Solitary
Gardening
Herbalism

- Folklore
- Ceremonial
- Divination
- Paganism
- Shamanism
- Alchemy
- Metaphysical
- Black magick
- Sigil magick
- Covens
- Sympathetic magick
- Internal manifestations
- Laws of Magick
- "Eight Words the Wiccan Rede Fulfill, And it Harm None, Do What Ye Will."
- Do unto others
- Threefold
- Accepting consequences to actions
- Law of karma
- Nature appreciation
- Giving back to the universe
- Doing your part
- Ways to prepare for successful spells
- Releasing fear and letting go
- Belief and confidence in any spell performed
- Deciding intentions and desires
- Timing for casting spells
- Days of the week, month and year
- Time of day or night
- Moon phases
- Seasons
- Holidays and Sabbath
- Element and zodiac correspondence
- Days that hold significance to specific intentions
- Wrong times to cast spells
- Supplies prepared
- Deciding your witch's name for spell casting
- Wearing power stones and jewelry
- Making space for making magick

- Clearing the room for magick
- Embracing the privacy
- Making your own unique set up for casting spells
- Organizing your witch's cupboard
- Feng Shui
- Meanings of colors
- Sights, scents and sounds
- Blessing your sacred space
- Knowledge of the gods and goddesses
- Angels and spirit understanding
- Invocation
- The only way to be careful when invoking a spirit
- Dos and do nots
- Choosing the appropriate spirits to invoke
- Calling the corners
- Understanding the importance of the elements
- Knowledge of north, east, south and west
- Drawing a circle
- Energy enhancement
- Circle of protection
- Different ways to seal a circle
- Why you can't undo a spell
- The right words to say
- Addressing and contacting
- Opening lines
- The power of sound
- The power of tone
- When to ask and when to demand
- Chanting
- Auming
- Mantras
- Word creation and manifestations
- Sealing spells with "So mote it be!", "So bless it be!" and "As I will it, so shall it be!"

Writing your own words for personalized spells
Giving thanks
Rituals and ceremonies
Symbolism
The power in closing what has been opened
Remembering to express gratitude
Feasting and celebrating
Witnessing your magick in motion

Types of spells
Rituals and ceremonial magick
The god and the goddess
Celebrating the Sabbaths
Blessings
Spells to manifest wishes
Good luck with lucky charms
Good health with the holistic route
Manifestations
"Thought crystalizes into habit, and habit solidifies into circumstance."
Protection spells
Seal of Solomon
Banishing spells
Get rid of unwanted spirits
Banish negative people
Banish negative energy
Cleansings
To free the dead just like the living
Saging and smudging
Rejuvenating a cycle of energy flow
Spirit summoning and invoking
Lists of demons and angels
Contacting your spirit guides
Hexes
Understanding the threefold law will occur – determining if it's worth it

Spells to get revenge
Love magick
Sex magick
Bindings
Drawing down the moon
Weather manipulations

Candle Magick
Luck spells
Energy charging
Glamours
Wishing inside yourself
Sigils
Worship
Herbalism
Herbs and plants and Nature's essentials
Belladonna
Hemlock
Mugwort
Ginger
Sea salt
Rain water
Holy water
Rice
Menstrual blood
Cemetery dirt
Dragons or doves
Blood ink
Feathered quills
Charcoal
Sandalwood
White sage
Silver
Thyme

Potions
Oils and powders
Oils
Dragon's blood ink and oil
Planetary oils
Astrological signs
Frankincense
Myrrh
Jasmine
Lavender
Peppermint
Lemon
Heliotrope
Ginger

Mirror Magick
Seeing the future
Spirit boothing instructions

Divination
Tarot card reading
Palmistry
Astrology
Dowsing
Numerology
Channeling
Runes
Tea leaves
Water spells
Fire spells
Air spells
Earth spells
Wand Magick
Spells with stones and crystals
Stones and crystals
Agate: wealth
Amber: peace
Amethyst: psychic intuition and healing
Aquamarine: hope
Bloodstone: fire magic and strength
Citrine: money and prosperity
Diamond: prophetic purposes
Emerald: wealth
Garnet: sexuality
Hematite: protection
Jade: prosperity and good fortune
Jasper: wish fulfillment
Moonstone: wisdom and beauty
Obsidian: meditation and grounding
Onyx: the afterlife and marriage
Opal: clairvoyance
Pearl: beauty
Peridot: fame and healing, also inner strength
Quartz: healing, love and energy restoration
Rose Quartz: peace and love
Ruby: strength, love, sex magick and power
Sapphire: fertility and creativity
Selenite spiritual connection
Sodalite: faery connection
Sugilite: hidden truths

Tiger's eye: protection from negative forces
Topaz: mystical power and protection
Tourmaline: attraction
Turquoise: protection from psychic attack and hexes, also healing

Crystal gazing spells
The most well-known and historic spells
Shielding
Breaking hexes
Chants and magick words
Symbol magick
Creating your own spells and why it's the most powerful magick of all

Final tips and secrets
Never holding back
Determining how the spell can affect you and others
Snuffing candles instead of blowing them out
Explore your options
Don't use magick against others for power
Be creative
Be yourself
Accept other religions and practices with an open mind
Do not play God
Respect all forms of nature and work with it
Keep your inner child alive in your magick
Set a great example
Take pride in your spells and be thorough and precise
Be specific when you manifest into the universe
Be careful what you wish for!
Never abuse the beauty in your blessings

Never stop researching and gaining knowledge of the craft
Embrace the goddess within
Have fun and be joyful in your magick
Guide others on their spiritual paths
Make the world a better place with your magick and spellcasting

The End